SETTLING CANADA

TOM SMITH

CANADA

A PEOPLE'S HISTORY

THOMSON

NELSON

Australia   Canada   Mexico   Singapore   Spain   United Kingdom   United States

THOMSON

NELSON

Canada: A People's History
Settling Canada

Series Consultants
Donald Bogle, Don Quinlan

Author
Tom Smith

Director of Publishing
Beverley Buxton

General Manager, Social Studies, Business Studies, and Languages
Carol Stokes

Publisher, Social Studies
Doug Panasis

Managing Editor, Development
Karin Fediw

Product Manager
Nadia McIlveen

Senior Editor
Loralee Case

Editorial Coordinator
Amy Hingston

Copy Editor/Indexer:
Penny Hozy

Executive Director, Content and Media Production
Renate McCloy

Director, Content and Media Production
Lisa Dimson

Production Manager
Cathy Deak

Senior Production Coordinator
Kathrine Pummell

Interior and Cover Design
Fortunato Designs Inc.

Photo Research
Lisa Brant, Alene McNeill

Printer
Transcontinental Printing Inc.

Canadian Broadcasting Corporation Representative
Karen Bower

The authors and the publisher are grateful to the Canadian Broadcasting Corporation for its assistance in the preparation of this volume in the book series based on its 17-episode, bilingual television documentary series, *Canada: A People's History*. For more information about *Canada: A People's History*, please visit www.cbc.ca/history.

Canada: A People's History
© 2000, 2001 Canadian Broadcasting Corporation

Contents

INTRODUCTION

1717

Long ago, sailing across the Atlantic Ocean was dangerous. In France, people placed pictures of saints in churches to help travellers arrive safely. Why do you think people crossed the sea to North America in spite of the dangers? Why would people today make a dangerous journey to another land?

THE BIG IDEA

The explorers who came to North America over 500 years ago were the first European immigrants. When they arrived, they found that thousands of Aboriginal peoples already lived here. These people spoke many languages. They had many different cultures. These **diverse** peoples were the first inhabitants of Canada.

In time, French and English settlers added their cultures to this land. Later on, more immigrants from Britain and Europe came to live here, too. Together with the First Nations, they laid the foundations for the country that today is Canada.

TIMELINE

1500 Europeans begin to arrive in North America

1627 The fur trade begins in New France

1663 King Louis XIV takes control of New France

1665 1,200 French soldiers are sent to New France

1534 A French fort is founded at Trois-Rivières

1643 Only 350 people live in New France

1664 The French and the Iroquois sign a peace treaty

PICTURE THIS

Can you imagine what it would be like to leave your home and travel across the ocean to a new land? Imagine that you had to spend weeks at sea, crowded onto a cold, damp ship. Imagine being hungry and sick throughout the journey. Then you finally reach land, only to find out that you have to travel for many more months on foot through the wilderness. Many thoughts go through your mind. Where will you sleep? What will you eat? How will you *survive*?

Finally, you reach your destination and find—nothing! No towns, no farms, no homes—only forests and fields and streams. Now, after an exhausting journey, you have to clear the land to build your new home. How would you feel? What would you need to do to succeed in this new land?

This is what the early European settlers experienced when they came to British North America. Who were these settlers? What pushed them away from their homelands? What pulled them towards North America? What hardships did they face when they arrived? What challenges did they overcome? What role did they play in laying the foundations of Canada?

Throughout time, people have migrated from one place to another. Some people are pushed away from their homes. Other people are pulled towards another place. Sometimes both push factors and pull factors motivate people to migrate. What factors do you think might *push* people *away* from a place? What factors do you think might *pull* people *towards* a place?

TIMELINE

1701 1,300 First Nations people meet the French to discuss the Great Peace

1759 British troops attack Quebec

1775 American rebels attack Quebec

1756–1763 Britain and France wage the Seven Years War

1760 New France becomes a British colony

1776 The Thirteen Colonies declare independence from Britain

Clearing the land was one of many hardships the early settlers faced.

TIMELINE

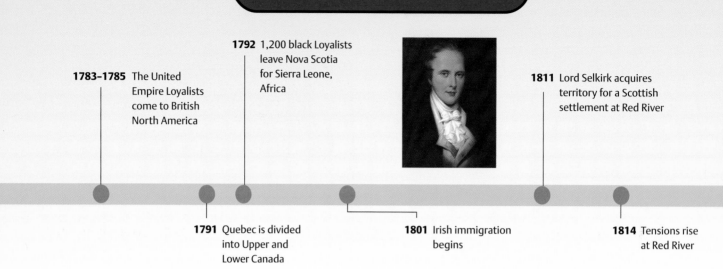

1783–1785 The United Empire Loyalists come to British North America

1792 1,200 black Loyalists leave Nova Scotia for Sierra Leone, Africa

1811 Lord Selkirk acquires territory for a Scottish settlement at Red River

1791 Quebec is divided into Upper and Lower Canada

1801 Irish immigration begins

1814 Tensions rise at Red River

The Origins of the First Peoples

Aboriginal peoples were the first inhabitants of North America. But how did they come to be here? Most historians and **archaeologists** believe that during the last Ice Age there was a land bridge across what is today the Bering Strait. They think that the First Peoples crossed this bridge from Asia into North America. But they cannot explain for certain *why* they came. Were they pushed away from Asia by war or famine or disease? Or were they pulled towards North America as they followed the herds of game that were their food supply?

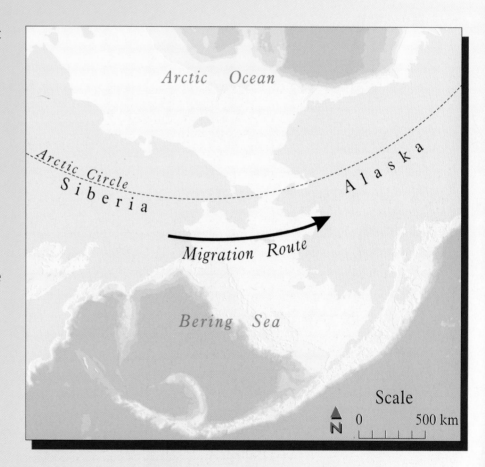

Did the First Peoples arrive in North America via a land bridge from Asia? Or have Aboriginal peoples always lived here, since time began? What do you think?

TIMELINE

1816 The incident at Seven Oaks leaves 20 settlers dead

1834 Slavery is abolished in the British Empire

1846–1849 The Potato Famine sweeps across Ireland

1818–1825 Disasters plague the Red River settlement

1841 The population in Ireland reaches 8 million

1847 A typhus epidemic hits Grosse Île, Quebec

Aboriginal peoples have a different idea about their origins. They believe they have lived in this land since time began. Their **creation stories** tell about their ancestors' beginnings here. These stories differ from one culture to another. But the stories of all Aboriginal cultures have one message in common: that North America is their homeland. The people know no other.

The creation stories of Aboriginal peoples involve a powerful connection with the natural world. Aboriginal stories like "Skywoman" reveal a world view in which people are part of the natural environment but are not in control of it.

SETTING THE SCENE

Aboriginal peoples were the first to live in the land we now call Canada. Each culture had its own unique society, with its own customs, traditions, and practices. The people knew how to use the natural resources that were available to them to survive and prosper.

Europeans began to arrive in North America around 1500. In the beginning, French fur traders set up their trading posts along the St. Lawrence River. In time, they were joined by settlers who came to farm the land. The French brought the culture, language, religion, and traditions of France with them. In many ways, life in New France reflected life in France.

When Europeans first reached North America, they had not even known the continent existed. Soon, though, the ships were transporting settlers who wanted to make the land their home.

Meanwhile, the English had established colonies up and down the Atlantic coast of North America. In Europe, England and France were rivals. They had fought many wars there. In 1756, this rivalry spilled over into North America. Britain gained control of New France. Then Britain lost its Thirteen Colonies after they declared their independence as the United States of America. Many British supporters left the United States and moved north into British North America. These United Empire Loyalists created a British presence in the French-speaking colony.

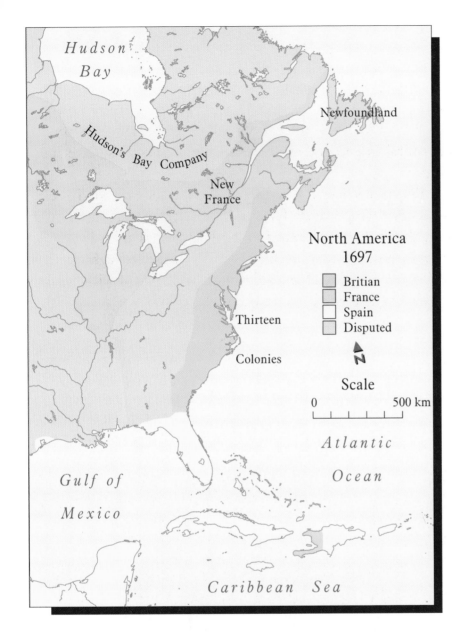

Hudson Bay

Newfoundland

Hudson's Bay Company

New France

North America 1697

Britian
France
Spain
Disputed

N

Scale

0   500 km

Thirteen

Colonies

Atlantic

Ocean

Gulf of

Mexico

Caribbean Sea

By 1697, Britain, France, and Spain had claimed large parts of North America as their own. What impact would this have on the original occupants of these lands?

In the early 1800s, British North America expanded west. Scottish settlers came to settle along the Red River in present-day Manitoba. These settlers faced many hardships. But they stayed on to create the first permanent settlement in the West. At the same time, thousands of Irish farmers came to British North America looking to start new lives.

Settling Canada examines the experiences of these immigrants. What were the factors that pushed them from their homeland? What were the factors that pulled them towards British North America? What were their experiences as they travelled here? What challenges did they face once they arrived? What did these immigrants have in common? What was unique about each of their experiences?

Telling Their Stories

THE SETTLERS OF NEW FRANCE

Starting new lives was difficult for the settlers. In time, though, they built strong communities. A Swedish **naturalist** named Pehr Kalm visited New France in the summer of 1749. He stayed for nine months. During this time, he learned much about New France and its people. He was very impressed with what he saw.

To learn about Kalm's impressions of New France, view the clip "1749 Was a Very Good Year" (*Canada: A People's History*, Episode 3, 10:27:56 to 10:31:08). How does Pehr Kalm describe life in New France? What evidence is there that the settlers were happy in their new home? What impressed Pehr Kalm most about the French settlers?

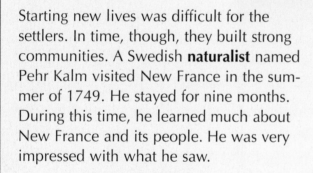

◀ Playback ▶

1. **What factors push people away from their homeland? What factors pull people towards another place? List your answers in a two-column organizer.**

2. **Have you ever moved from your home to a new and unfamiliar place? What challenges did you face? How did you feel?**

3. **What factors do you think pull immigrants towards Canada today?**

4. **With your family, discuss the major push and pull factors that influenced you or your ancestors to come to Canada.**

Chapter I

Settlers of New France

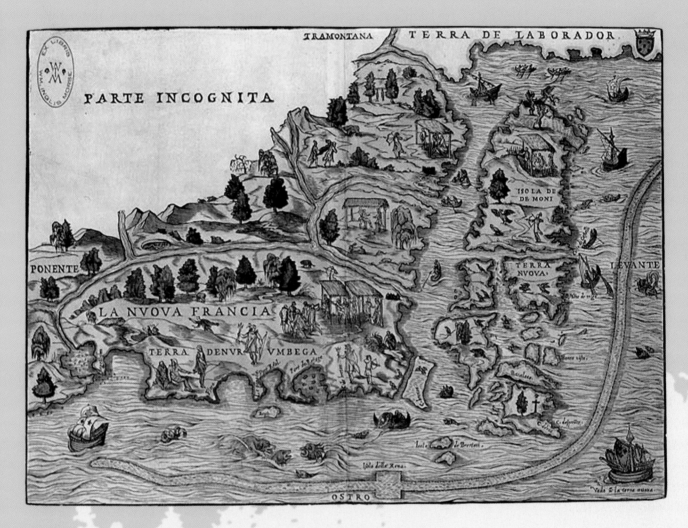

The French were the first to settle in the place we now call Canada. In the beginning, New France had only a few small settlements scattered along the St. Lawrence River. But the king of France dreamed of building a great colony. He wanted to create an empire across North America. To build an empire, though, New France needed to grow. How could France build its tiny colony?

During the seventeenth century, France was the most powerful empire in Europe. The French king, Louis XIII, wanted to make sure he remained the most powerful monarch in Europe. He was more interested in fighting costly wars than in spending time or money in New France. Instead, the king gave a group of fur traders control over the colony.

This map is from the sixteenth century. It shows the beginnings of the French colony in North America. Why do you think the kings and queens of Europe wanted to have great empires?

From the Sources

As time went on, the supply of furs in New France began to dwindle. The French fur traders wanted to move further inland to trade for furs with the Aboriginal peoples who lived there. But the Iroquois blocked the French from gaining access to these lands. Soon, there were hardly any furs at the trading posts.

The store in Ville-Marie has not bought a single beaver skin…over the last year. In Trois-Rivières, the few stragglers to be found thereabouts have been put to work fortifying the place. The store in Quebec reeks of poverty. The Iroquois have shut down the entire trade in beavers, which has always been one of the great resources of the country.

A Jesuit priest

Seigneurs lived in large manor homes on their estates. It was usually the job of the *habitants* to clear the *seigneurs'* land and help build their houses.

A Fur Trade Monopoly

In 1627, the Company of One Hundred Associates was given a **monopoly** over the fur trade. In return, they were to build settlements in New France. But the fur traders were not interested in settlements. What they really wanted was to make money—and lots of it—in the fur trade.

Still, the Company of One Hundred Associates knew they had to do something if they wanted to keep control over the fur trade. So they encouraged wealthy merchants to take on the task of settlement. They gave them sections of land, called *seigneuries*, along the St. Lawrence River. These merchants then became the landlords, or *seigneurs*. Their job was to rent out plots of land to farmers called *habitants*.

These attempts to build settlements in New France failed, though. By 1643, only 350 people lived in the colony. Without more settlers, it was hard for the fur traders to expand their business further inland. There were also not enough settlers to defend the colony against the powerful Iroquois nation. Relations between the Iroquois and the French were hostile. Over 100 years earlier, the explorer Jacques Cartier had kidnapped some Iroquois people and taken them back to France. Since then, the Iroquois had not trusted the French. They also distrusted France's trading partners, the Algonquin and the

Huron. The rivalry between these groups led to many Iroquois raids against the French trading posts at Montreal (Ville Marie) and Trois-Rivières. Something had to be done to end the raids. Otherwise, it might be the end of the fur trade.

The settlers in New France were worried. They knew that if they did not receive help from home their colony would not survive. They decided to send someone to France to plead to King Louis XIV to help them. Louis had a great dream of ruling over a rich and powerful empire. He knew that if he lost New France, it would be hard to fulfil that dream. So Louis ended the fur trade monopoly and took control of New France himself. With the help of a government minister named Jean-Baptiste Colbert, Louis XIV set out to build New France.

GOVERNMENT IN NEW FRANCE

The first thing the king needed to do was set up a government. Louis modelled the government in New France after the governments of the French provinces. The Sovereign Council was the ruling body. Power was shared by three people: the governor general, the *intendant*, and the bishop.

The governor general was usually a noble. He represented the king directly and was the military leader of the colony. He supervised the local governors in Montreal, Trois-Rivières, and Port Royal. He also dealt with the leaders of First Nations and the colonies of other empires.

The fort of Trois-Rivières was founded in 1534. Over the next 100 years, it grew into a trading post. What advantages do you think its location had for the French?

Louis XIV and the Ancien Régime

In the seventeenth century, France was ruled under a system known as the Ancien Régime. This gave the monarch total power. To help him rule, the monarch gave certain powers to important nobles. Since the nobles received their authority from the king, they had total power, too. What power do you think average citizens had?

Louis XIV had absolute power in France. He declared *l'Etat c'est moi*—"I am the State."

The *intendant* was usually a professional man, often a lawyer. He was responsible for laws and money matters as well as the day-to-day running of New France. He held a lot of power over the daily lives of the settlers.

The bishop was in charge of religious life in the colony. He ran the affairs of the Roman Catholic Church. He also led the Church's efforts to convert Aboriginal peoples to Christianity.

The governor general, the *intendant,* and the bishop were supported by several councilors. These were important merchants and nobles who were appointed to the Sovereign Council. What does this system tell you about the role of the average settlers in the government of New France?

KEEPING THE PEACE

If they were going to build New France, the government knew they would need many more settlers. Before they could expand the colony, though, they had to end the conflict with the Iroquois. So in 1665, a troop of 1,200 soldiers known as the *Carignan-Salières* was sent to the colony. Their mission was to attack the Iroquois. But the troops were unprepared for the harsh winters of New France. On their first raid, over 400 soldiers froze to death without ever seeing any Iroquois.

The drummers of the *Carignan-Salières* wore the colours of their commander. Their coat of arms was painted on the side of their drums. The drummer's job was to relay the commander's orders through drum rolls.

In the fall of 1665, the *Carignan-Salières* launched a second attack against the Iroquois. But when they reached the Iroquois villages, they found them deserted. The French troops then burned the villages to the ground. With winter approaching, they returned to Quebec. Now the Iroquois faced a harsh winter without their homes and villages. So the Iroquois and the French agreed to sign a peace treaty.

FROM SOLDIERS TO SETTLERS

With peace in New France, the *Carignan-Salières* were ready to return home in 1667. But the king wanted the soldiers to remain in the colony. So he offered land grants, money, and supplies to the soldiers if they stayed. The plan worked. Over 400 troops settled in New France. Life in the colony was hard. But the soldiers found greater freedom and the chance for a better life than in France.

Telling Their Stories

KONDIARONK

In the 1680s, conflicts between the Iroquois and the Huron and the Algonquin once again threatened the colony. France's allies, the Huron and the Algonquin, wanted the French to support them against the Iroquois. But France wanted peace. In 1701, 1,300 members of the First Nations met with French officials in Montreal. Kondiaronk was a great chief of the Huron Nation. He was one of France's strongest allies and one of the most important speakers during the talks for the Great Peace.

View the clip "The Great Peace" (*Canada: A People's History*, Episode 3, 10:22:16 to 10:27:39). Why do you think Aboriginal peoples agreed to meet with the French to discuss peace? Why do you think Kondiaronk's support for peace was so important? What does the funeral that was held for Kondiaronk suggest about him?

Marriage in New France

For New France to grow and prosper, the male settlers and soldiers needed wives and families. In 1663, the French government began a campaign to recruit young women from across France to settle in the colony. Most of these women came from poor families or were orphans. Without a **dowry**, they had little chance of marrying a man who could provide them with a comfortable life. So the government obtained money from the royal treasury to provide each woman with a dowry. As a result, the women became known as *les filles du roi*—"the King's daughters."

A few of *les filles du roi* came from wealthy families. These women usually married officers or important men in the colony. But the best quality for a *fille du roi* to possess was the ability to be a good farmer.

Over the next ten years, more than 800 *filles du roi* settled in New France. Some found the rugged pioneer life too harsh and returned to France. But most of the women stayed on and worked hard. They played an important role in building the colony of New France.

◀ Playback ▶

1. How did Louis XIV plan to expand the colony?

2. (a) What factors do you think pushed the settlers to leave France?
   (b) What factors do you think pulled the settlers towards New France?

3. Assume the role of either a soldier in the *Carignan-Salières* or a *fille du roi*. Write a one-page letter home to France describing your feelings about life in the colony and your hopes for the future.

THE SEIGNEURIAL SYSTEM

The social structure in New France was made up of three groups: the nobles, the clergy, and the commoners. Most colonists— 95 percent—were commoners. About two-thirds of these were peasant farmers who worked the land on the *seigneuries*. These farmers were called *les habitants*. The rest of the commoners were merchants, labourers, craftworkers, and servants.

Being a *seigneur* had many benefits. *Seigneurs* were often given important jobs in government, the military, and the fur trade. In return for these honours, they rented their land to the *habitants*. Usually, many *habitant* families worked on one *seigneury* in order to provide a good income for the *seigneur*. Unlike the peasant farmers in France, though, the *habitants* did not have to serve as soldiers to protect the *seigneurs* and their land. They had a legal contract that outlined what obligations they had to their landlord.

THE HABITANTS' HOMES

The *habitants'* homes were usually small and built from the materials that were available to them. Wood was used to build homes and barns most often. There was always a large supply of wood after the land was cleared! Wood also provided good protection against the cold winter winds.

Land Along the River

In New France, the dense forests made it hard to travel over land. Therefore, the settlers relied on the river as their main transportation route. Homes and barns on a *seigneury* were located beside the river. This gave the settlers easy access to water for drinking and washing.

The pattern of land distribution in New France can still be seen along the St. Lawrence River today. What pattern can you identify? What were the advantages of a land system that was centred along a major river?

Some homes had thatched roofs. These were similar to the ones many peasant homes had in France. Other homes had roofs made from wooden shingles. Roofs were built with a steep peak so that the snow could slide off in the winter. These peaked roofs created a large attic inside. If the *habitants* did not have a barn, they used this space to store grain and hay. This also helped to insulate the home in winter. Once a barn was built, the *habitants* often turned the attic into a second floor of bedrooms.

Many homes had two main fireplaces, one at each end of the building. To keep the heat indoors, stone chimneys were built inside the home rather than outside. Windows were small to prevent strong drafts. Since glass was expensive, the *habitants* used oiled paper or cloth that allowed light to shine through but helped to keep insects out. Windows also had shutters that could be closed during bad weather.

The settlers built their barns in the style of the barns in France. A barn was long and rectangular. The first floor housed the livestock. A ramp led to the second floor, which was used to store grain and hay.

A Time for Celebration

The homes of the *habitants* were the main social centres in New France. The people gathered at their homes to celebrate weddings and christenings. Although the *habitants* worked hard on their farms, they took the time to enjoy social celebrations.

To celebrate popular feasts, the *habitants* sometimes gathered at the manor house of the *seigneur* or in the village square.

Farming on a Seigneury

The first job for the *habitants* was to clear the land. It took several workers an entire year to clear 10 hectares of dense forest. Once the land was cleared, though, the crops flourished in the rich soil.

Some land was used for growing wheat and barley. The settlers also learned how to grow corn and pumpkins from Aboriginal farmers. Land that was not suited for growing crops was used as grazing pasture for livestock. Aboriginal peoples also taught the *habitants* how to hunt and cook game.

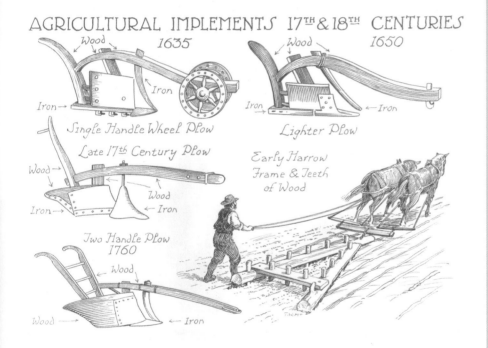

AGRICULTURAL IMPLEMENTS 17TH & 18TH CENTURIES

Wood 1635
Iron
Iron
Single Handle Wheel Plow
Late 17th Century Plow
Wood
Wood
Iron
Iron
Two Handle Plow 1760
Wood
Wood
Iron

Wood 1650
Iron
Iron
Lighter Plow
Early Harrow Frame & Teeth of Wood

In France, the soils were often wet and heavy. Conditions in New France were similar, so the *habitants* used similar farm tools. Ploughs were used to till the soil so that it could dry out. Tools made farming a little easier, but it was still hard work.

Most *habitants* in New France were successful farmers. They didn't grow enough to send extra crops back to France, but they had enough to feed their families. What the *habitants* could not produce on the farm, they got from hunting and fishing. This meant that most *habitant* families were **self-sufficient**. They had more food, warmer clothing, and better houses than farmers in France did.

The Coureurs de Bois

The *coureurs de bois* were independent young men who were eager for adventure and fortune. They lived among the Aboriginal peoples as they trapped and traded furs. These young men lived off the land. They often risked their lives as they searched for the best furs that would bring the highest prices. Some colonists disapproved of the free-spirited lifestyle of the *coureurs de bois*.

Do you think life as a *coureur de bois* would have been an adventure? Why or why not?

INDUSTRIES IN NEW FRANCE

In the early days, the fur trade was the major industry in New France. Once the French and the Iroquois reached a peace agreement, the fur trade was able to expand. French fur traders travelled further west with their Aboriginal partners in search of the best furs. The furs were then taken back to the trading posts. From there, they were shipped to France, where the beaver pelts were made into the most fashionable hats in Europe! But only a few fur traders became wealthy from the fur trade. Most of the money went to the merchants and fur-trading companies back in France.

King Louis XIV wanted New France to expand its economy beyond the fur trade, though. He wanted to create **primary industries** that would support the French empire. First, his government planned to develop the fishing industry in the Gulf of St. Lawrence. But there was no local supply of salt to preserve the fish. This meant that shiploads of salt had to be brought over from France. This made the cost of importing the fish to France too high. So they looked for other resources in New France that could be used to help build the French empire.

France was eager to compete with the powerful Dutch and British shipping fleets. To do this, they needed a strong ship-building industry. New France was covered with vast forests that could provide all the timber they needed to build the ships. But the cost of logging and shipping was too high. As a result, France gave up its attempts to build its shipping industry. For the time being, New France was destined to remain a farming colony.

The first shipyard in New France opened in 1739. It was located near the mouth of the St. Charles River near present-day Quebec City.

◀ Playback ▶

1. Review the roles of the governor general, the *intendant*, and the bishop in New France. How important do you think it was for them to work together? If you lived in New France, which job would you have wanted? Why?

2. In what ways were the lives of the *habitants* similar to the lives of peasants living in France? In what ways were they different?

3. Write a letter to your family back in France telling about your life as a *habitant* living on a *seigneury*.

4. What evidence is there that settling in New France was a good choice for poor French peasant farmers?

History in Action   Biography of the Past

The Back Story

History is filled with the voices of many people from many different backgrounds. One way to help us understand history is to read about the real-life experiences of the people who lived in the past. When we read people's stories, history becomes more personal. We see what people's lives were like. We may even find connections with our own lives.

The biography you are about to read tells the story of one young French settler and his wife. As you read it, think about how these people may have felt about the events that took place in their lives. How might you have felt if these events had happened to you?

Soldiers like Pierre Jamme dit Carrière were needed to fight back English and Aboriginal forces at Quebec.

The Goal

In this activity, you are to create a history bio-card. Your bio-card will highlight the key events in the life of Pierre Jamme dit Carrière. Once you have completed your bio-card, view the first half of Episode 3 in *Canada: A People's History*. As you watch, identify another person who lived in New France. Then use the information in the video and some further research to write a biography of this person.

The Steps

1. Read the biography of Pierre Jamme dit Carrière on pages 21–22. As you read, jot down five to ten key points about his life.
2. Design a history bio-card—something like a hockey card—to summarize the key events in his life. Be sure to include important dates.
3. Draw a visual for your bio-card. This could be a picture of what you think Pierre might have looked like or of an event in his life.
4. Choose another person who lived in New France during this time. Do further research about this person. Then write a brief biography describing the key events in this person's life.

Evaluating Your Work

These are the criteria you should think about as you complete your work. Your work should:

- show that you have read the biography carefully by the notes you have made about Pierre's life
- demonstrate your creativity and imagination in designing your bio-card
- present a visual element that shows some aspect of Pierre Jamme dit Carrière's life
- show that you have researched the life of another person who lived in New France

THE STORY OF PIERRE JAMME DIT CARRIÈRE

Pierre Jamme dit Carrière was born into a family of peasant farmers in rural France in 1662. When he was in his early twenties, the French military was recruiting men to go to New France to help end the conflict between the Iroquois and the French. Pierre decided to join. On April 26, 1687, he boarded one of eight troop ships sailing across the Atlantic to New France.

The voyage took 33 days. During this time a measles **epidemic** broke out. Seventeen men died. Another 130 had to go to the hospital when they arrived at the colony. In spite of the measles outbreak, the colonists welcomed the troops. They knew the king was going to help them after all.

The *habitants* invited the soldiers to stay in their homes until they were needed for military duty. The soldiers helped the *habitants* with their harvests and daily chores. This helped them adjust to life in the colony. They also met potential brides.

Pierre was sent to a military base in Lachine. In 1688, he met and married Marie Madeleine Barbary, the daughter of a former soldier and a *fille du roi*. However, Pierre's life took a terrible turn the following year. On August 5, 1689, the village of Lachine was raided by the Iroquois. Marie's parents were killed. Pierre survived, but Marie was captured. For the next twelve years, no one knew where she was. Although Pierre searched, he was unable to find his wife.

Following the raid on Lachine, the governor of New France was ordered to return to France. He was replaced by Count Frontenac, who had been governor of the colony once before. He opened up peace talks with all the First Nations of New France. It took ten years, but in 1701 the Great Peace Treaty was signed in Montreal.

One of the terms of the treaty was that all those who had been captured and held prisoner had to be released and returned to their families. Pierre was finally reunited with his wife. Between 1701 and 1716, Pierre and Marie had seven children. Then, Marie died shortly after the birth of their last child. Pierre continued to live in Lachine until his death in 1740.

In the Great Peace Treaty, France secured an alliance with Aboriginal peoples. Why is this document unique?

CHAPTER 2

THE LOYALISTS

Between 1756 and 1763, Britain and France waged the Seven Years War in Europe. In 1758, however, the war crossed the Atlantic into New France. Britain sent thousands of troops to battle the French for control of the colony. In 1758, the fortress of Louisbourg fell to the British. Then, in 1759, British troops attacked Quebec. The French stronghold quickly fell. When it was over, New France was in British hands.

The war had expanded Britain's empire, especially in North America. Now Britain needed a large army to keep the peace among the English colonists in the Thirteen Colonies, the French colonists in Quebec, and the Aboriginal peoples. But the cost of the Seven Years War had almost emptied the British treasury. They needed money to maintain a North American army. Where would the money come from?

This painting shows a group of Loyalists arriving at the place that would become Saint John, New Brunswick. As you read this chapter, what evidence can you find to suggest that the Loyalists laid the foundations of English Canada?

No Taxation without Representation!

Britain's solution was simple: they would raise money by increasing taxes in the colonies. That was not good news for the people in the Thirteen Colonies. They already thought their taxes were too high. They bitterly resented plans to raise them even higher. But what they resented even more was the fact that they paid taxes to the British government but had no say in the British Parliament. In protest, the colonists proclaimed *"No Taxation without Representation!"* It would become the rallying cry for a revolution.

People in the Thirteen Colonies found many ways to oppose Britain's tax policies.

The Tensions Mount

When Britain passed the Quebec Act in 1774, relations with the Thirteen Colonies were already tense. But the Quebec Act made matters worse. It expanded the boundaries of Quebec to include parts of the Ohio and Mississippi valleys. This ended any hopes the Thirteen Colonies had about expanding into the West. The colonists protested, but Britain paid no attention.

Rebels on the Rise

The people of the Thirteen Colonies were becoming more and more impatient with their British rulers. A group of rebel

The Boston Tea Party

Britain placed taxes on **staple** goods, including paper, sugar, and tea. In Boston, the colonists wanted to show Britain that they had had enough. In the dark of night on December 16, 1773, a group of colonists disguised as Iroquois slipped down to Boston harbour. There they invaded a British ship and hurled chests of tea into the water! This became known as the Boston Tea Party.

Americans launched an uprising against Britain. They tried to persuade the Quebec colonists to join them. But the *Canadiens* were not interested. Although they were no longer ruled by France, they had found that life under British rule was not much different. Then there was the question of the Americans themselves. The *Canadiens* distrusted their neighbours. The Americans had made it clear that they thought French culture and the Catholic Church were inferior to their own way of life and religion. So the colonists of Quebec decided to remain **neutral**.

The Americans decided to fight Britain by attacking Quebec. In the fall of 1775, American rebels moved into the colony. They quickly captured Montreal. Then, in the middle of a raging blizzard on December 31, 1775, the Americans attacked Quebec City. The British were able to fend off the attack. Many American rebels were killed. But the survivors launched a **siege** on Quebec City. Supplies and communications were cut off. The rebels were able to surround the city until the spring of 1776. Then, more British troops arrived. Soon, the Americans were forced to retreat.

The Quebec Act

The *Canadiens* remained neutral mainly because of the Quebec Act. The act restored the colony to its former size. It also recognized that Britain would not try to **assimilate** the French-speaking colonists into the English way of life. The French colonists felt their rights were protected under British rule. They were not so sure the Americans would protect their rights, though.

Many colonists joined British troops to defend Quebec against the American invasion.

By 1776, tensions between British forces and American rebels had reached the breaking point. On July 4th, the Thirteen Colonies declared their independence. But the British government did not plan to let its colonies go without a fight. The two sides battled each other in the War of Independence. The conflict lasted for several years. Finally, Britain knew the fight was lost. In 1783, Britain recognized the independent United States of America.

THE LOYALISTS SIDE WITH BRITAIN

By 1776, people of many different cultures lived in the Thirteen Colonies. Not all of them sided with the rebels. Thousands of European immigrants remained loyal to Britain. So did many black slaves and Aboriginal peoples. Those who remained loyal to Britain were known as the United Empire Loyalists.

The Loyalists responded to the War of Independence in different ways. Some took direct action to support Britain and fought alongside British soldiers. Others worked behind the scenes. They spied on rebel meetings and **sabotaged** rebel camps. Still others decided to ride out the war. They hoped the American rebels would be defeated. Then life would return to normal.

As the war dragged on, it became impossible for anyone to stay on the sidelines. Loyalists who remained in the Thirteen

The Loyalists' Motives

Not all Loyalists shared the same reasons for supporting the British. Some were truly loyal to Britain and supported the British monarch. Others were afraid that **democracy** would create a **mob mentality**. Still others believed the British would win the war. They simply wanted to be on the winning side.

American rebels punished many Loyalists by hanging them on display in the town squares.

Colonies were branded as **traitors** by the rebels. Their homes, farms, and businesses were seized and destroyed. There was physical violence, too. Some Loyalists were coated with tar and feathers. Then they were paraded through the town streets, where the people inflicted further punishment.

The violence forced many Loyalists to escape to safety in British North America. Most were forced to leave their belongings behind. They arrived in British North America with little more than the clothes on their backs and the hope of starting a new life.

More than 50,000 Loyalists came to British North America. But what kind of life did they come to? What support did they receive from the British government? What hardships did they face in the remote, unsettled lands of the British colonies?

THE LOYALISTS COME TO NOVA SCOTIA

When 40,000 Loyalists settled in Nova Scotia between 1783 and 1785, they tripled the population of the small colony. The Loyalists expected the British government to repay them for the things they had lost at the hands of the Americans. They had been promised free land and supplies to help them start their new lives. But Britain was slow to fulfil its promises. As a result, the Loyalists had to look after themselves. Some found their new life too hard. They left aboard the relief ships that arrived in the spring. Many others stayed, however. Through determination and hard work, these Loyalists built strong communities.

Who Were the Loyalists?

The Loyalists came from all walks of life. They were white, black, and Aboriginal. They were British and European. They were wealthy landowners and poor farmers. They were lawyers and labourers, merchants and mariners, soldiers and slaves. But while they came from different backgrounds, they had one thing in common: they were all against the revolution.

The arrows show the routes the Loyalists took after leaving the United States. The shaded areas on the main map show where the Loyalists settled in British North America. The inset map shows black Loyalist settlements in Nova Scotia.

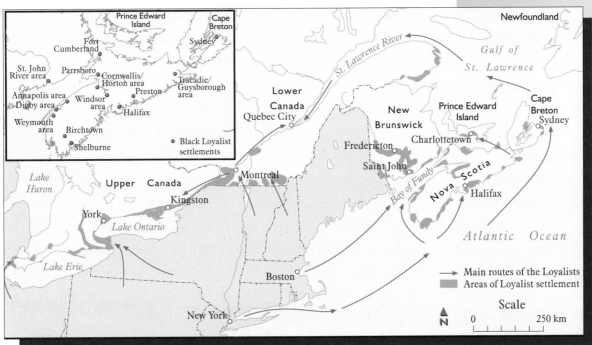

THE SETTLEMENT AT SHELBURNE

The first wave of Loyalists settled in the southern tip of Nova Scotia at Shelburne in May 1783. When they arrived, they expected to find land lots, supplies, and help from the colonial government. Instead, they found chaos and confusion! There were no surveyed land lots. There were no supplies. There was no help from the colonial government, located far away in Halifax. Many Loyalists were disappointed. Britain was not living up to the promises it had made to them.

At first, the Loyalists were forced to live in simple tents or crude log cabins. With winter coming, though, they desperately needed warm shelter and a stockpile of supplies. But with a steady stream of people arriving at Shelburne, the tiny community could not build housing fast enough. Many people were forced to spend the winter on board the ships that had brought them there or in public buildings.

Still, the harsh conditions did not prevent the Loyalists from coming, and the colony quickly grew. Shelburne soon became a boomtown. Shops and businesses opened up to provide supplies and services to the newcomers. By 1784, Shelburne's population had soared to 10,000. For a brief time, this Loyalist community was the largest city in North America!

The boom did not last, though. After a few years, most of the settlers had grown tired of the hardships and had abandoned Shelburne. Some returned to the United States. Others resettled in other parts of Nova Scotia and in Quebec.

THE LOYALISTS CREATE NEW BRUNSWICK

Two more waves of Loyalist settlers arrived in Nova Scotia in the summer and fall of 1783. They settled on the western shores of the Bay of Fundy. By the end of the year, there were over 15,000 Loyalists there. The community was overcrowded, though. So a group of about 2,000 settlers decided to move inland. They settled in a place they called St. Anne's.

At St. Anne's, the settlers began to prepare for winter. But driving winds and heavy snows came early that year. There was no time to build proper housing. In desperation, the settlers built makeshift tents, with only the earth as a floor. Worse still, there was a shortage of food and other supplies. Many people did not survive the first winter.

Despite these early hardships, though, the Loyalists stayed on to build strong communities. All along the St. John River and the Bay of Fundy, towns named St. Andrew, Saint John, and Frederick Town reflected their strong British ties. Yet the colonists still felt too distant from the government in Halifax. They decided they needed their own colony and their own government. Britain agreed. In June 1784, Nova Scotia was divided in half and a new colony was created: New Brunswick.

In May 1783, 2000 Loyalists settled along the western shores of the Bay of Fundy. This settlement became Saint John, New Brunswick.

From the Sources

Hannah Ingraham and her family were Loyalists. During the War of Independence, the rebels took away their farm in New York State after her father joined the British forces. After the war, in 1783, they set sail for Nova Scotia to claim the land that was promised to the Loyalists. Hannah and her family settled at St. Anne's in the winter of 1783–1784.

It was a sad sick time after we landed in Saint John. We had to live in tents. The government gave them to us and rations too. It was just at the first snow then and the melting snow and the rain would soak up into our beds as we lay. Mother got so chilled and developed rheumatism and was never well afterward.

We lived in a tent at St. Anne's until father got a house ready….There was no floor laid, no windows, no chimney, no door, but we had a roof at least. A good fire was blazing and mother had a big loaf of bread and she boiled a kettle of water and put a good piece of butter in a pewter bowl. We toasted the bread and all sat around the bowl and at our breakfast that morning mother said: "Thank God we are no longer in dread of having shots fired through our house." This is the sweetest meal I ever tasted for many a day.

Freedom for All?

Britain's offer of freedom applied only to the black slaves of rebel colonists. The slaves of white Loyalists remained enslaved. When wealthy white Loyalists settled in Shelburne, they brought slaves with them. Some of these slaves escaped and joined the free black Loyalists. The black Loyalists were not always able to enjoy their freedom, though. They always had to worry that they would be kidnapped by the slave traders who sailed around the coast of Nova Scotia.

THE BLACK LOYALISTS

The story of the black Loyalists is one of hope and tragedy. When the War of Independence began, there were over 500,000 black slaves in the Thirteen Colonies. Britain saw the black slaves as potential allies in the war. They needed the men to fight alongside British troops and to work behind the scenes supporting the army. The British government promised "Freedom and a Farm" to any black slaves who escaped and pledged their loyalty to Britain. Over 100,000 black people saw the chance to escape from slavery. They moved north to join the British army. It was a time of hope for the former slaves. They believed they were free to start new lives in a new land.

THE SETTLEMENT AT BIRCHTOWN

While Britain was slow to help the white Loyalists, things were even worse for the black Loyalists. One of the first black Loyalist settlements was located on the outskirts of Shelburne, Nova Scotia. (See the map on page 27.) The coastal location offered spectacular scenery, but it provided little else for the black settlers. The land was rocky in some places and swampy in others. Nowhere was there any land suitable for farming.

Over 1,500 black Loyalists settled in this community. They called it Birchtown, after General Samuel Birch, who had brought them to the colony. Once there, they were forced to look after themselves. With little money and almost no supplies, they could build only simple one-room shelters with bark roofs and stone floors. There was little furniture—perhaps a bed, a table, and a stool. Since most black Loyalists were used to living in the warmer climates of the southern United States, they did not have warm clothing for a northern winter.

The British army often dug pit houses for shelter while they were on the march. Black soldiers learned how to build these houses when they served with British forces. Some black Loyalists built pit houses when they first arrived in Nova Scotia. Holes in the ground like this one were covered with roofs made from tree trunks and canvas.

Birch Certificates

After the War of Independence, black Loyalists wanted the British government to guarantee their freedom. General Samuel Birch helped black Loyalists travel from New York to Nova Scotia. He issued certificates to the black Loyalists as proof of their freedom.

A Birch Certificate guaranteed the black Loyalists a safe journey out of the United States.

NEW-YORK, 21st April 1783.

THIS is to certify to whomsoever it may concern, that the Bearer hereof _Cato Ramsay_ a Negro, resorted to the British Lines, in consequence of the Proclamations of Sir William Howe, and Sir Henry Clinton, late Commanders in Chief in America; and that the said Negro has hereby his Excellency Sir Guy Carleton's Permission to go to Nova-Scotia, or wherever else _He_ may think proper. ——

By Order of Brigadier General Birch,

Most black Loyalists were unable to earn a living from farming. Either they had no land or the land they had was unsuitable for growing crops. Many black Loyalists were skilled workers, though. They were blacksmiths, bakers, tailors, carpenters, and shoemakers. Others were ministers, teachers, soldiers, and sailors. These workers were able to earn a modest living. But they were paid much less than white workers for doing the

This is a watercolour of a black woodcutter at Shelburne in 1788. It is believed to be the first image of a Nova Scotian of black heritage.

Unfair Land Distribution

By 1786, most white Loyalists had received their land from Britain. But two years later, most black Loyalists were still waiting. Furthermore, the few black settlers who had received land found that their lots were only half the size of the lots the white settlers received.

same jobs. This led to Canada's first race riot in July 1784. A mob of white workers was angry because the lower-paid black workers got most of the jobs. They tried to chase the black workers out of Shelburne. During the riots, many homes in the community were destroyed.

Black Loyalists who did not have a trade were forced to work as **tenant farmers** for white Loyalists. The black farmers cleared and farmed the land, then gave half the money from the sale of the crops to the owners. The tenant families were allowed to keep the other half to buy food and more seed for next year's crop. Being a tenant farmer, however, was much like being a slave.

By 1792, many black Loyalists had had enough of the hostility they had faced in Nova Scotia. When they had the chance to resettle in Sierra Leone in Africa, 1,200 black Loyalists decided to leave. On January 15, 1792, they boarded a fleet of 15 ships sailing out of Halifax and left the colony behind for good. Not everyone left, though. More than two-thirds of the black Loyalists stayed in Nova Scotia. They worked hard to build strong and proud communities.

◄ Playback ►

1. (a) Who were the United Empire Loyalists?
    (b) What factors pushed the Loyalists out of the United States?
    (c) What factors pulled the Loyalists towards British North America?

2. What problems did the Loyalists face in Nova Scotia?

3. (a) Who were the black Loyalists?
    (b) What factors pushed the black Loyalists out of the United States?
    (c) What factors pulled the black Loyalists towards British North America?

4. In what ways were the experiences of the white Loyalists in Shelburne different from the experiences of the black Loyalists in Birchtown?

5. Imagine you are a Loyalist settler. What would have been the most difficult challenge for you to overcome?

THE LOYALISTS IN QUEBEC

During the War of Independence, some Loyalists settled in **refugee** camps in Quebec. After the war, they wanted to remain in the colony. At the time, most of the French colonists lived along the eastern part of the St. Lawrence River. The territory west of Montreal was largely unsettled. Most of the Loyalists decided that this was where they wanted to make their homes.

At first, the Loyalists presented a problem for the governor of Quebec. He felt it would disrupt the colony if the English Loyalists lived alongside the French colonists. How could he solve this problem?

The Treaty of Paris that ended the War of Independence helped the governor find a solution. The treaty gave all of the lands west of the Mississippi to the United States. This cleared the way for the Americans to expand into the west. But how would this affect Quebec? What would happen to the fur trade now that Britain had betrayed the Six Nations at the peace talks? How could the demands of the Loyalists be met? How could Quebec defend its western frontier against an American attack? The answer seemed obvious. To keep the colony secure, Quebec would have to expand westward, too.

Butler's Rangers

In 1777, Butler's Rangers joined forces with Aboriginal soldiers from the Six Nations, who were under the command of Mohawk chief Joseph Brant. The two forces waged long and bloody campaigns against the American rebels.

After the war, Butler's Rangers were rewarded for helping Britain. They received land grants along the west bank of the Niagara River. The Six Nations were promised land, too. But in the treaty that ended the war, Britain betrayed the Six Nations. It gave all land west of the Mississippi River—land that had been promised to the Six Nations—to the Americans.

Joseph Brant demanded that the British give the Six Nations other land. They finally received 275,000 hectares north of Lake Erie. In 1784, Brant and 1,800 members of the Six Nations settled along the shores of the Grand River.

The Six Nations called their new home Brant's Ford. Today, we know the town as Brantford.

The best land lots were the ones along the shores of the lake and river. To be fair to everyone, the Loyalists drew tickets out of a hat to see where their lots would be located. This is where the term "lottery" came from.

In 1783 and 1784, over 10,000 Loyalists settled in the western part of the colony. Many chose to live along the north shore of Lake Ontario and on the Niagara Peninsula. The Loyalists were used to British laws and customs, though. They were afraid they would lose these traditions living in a French colony. So they asked Britain to create a separate English colony. Britain agreed. In 1791, the Constitutional Act divided Quebec into Upper Canada (Ontario) and Lower Canada (Quebec). The seeds of a new nation had been planted.

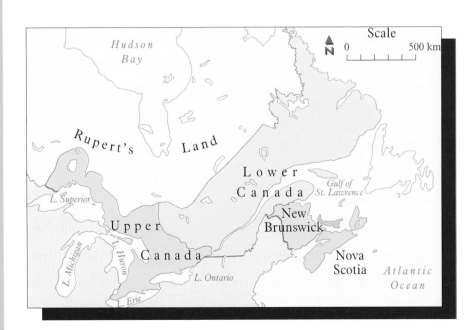

The division of Quebec created two distinct societies in Upper and Lower Canada.

Telling Their Stories

JOSEPH BRANT

Over 2,000 Loyalists were Aboriginal peoples. The most famous Aboriginal Loyalist was a Mohawk chief and British army captain named Joseph Brant. Brant was a powerful ally for Britain. He led his troops in many battles against the American rebels. But when the British betrayed the Six Nations at the peace talks, Brant was shocked and dismayed.

View the clip "Brave New Worlds" (*Canada: A People's History*, Episode 5, 10:54:11 to 10:56:35). Why do you think the British betrayed Brant and the Six Nations at the peace talks? Do you think they were right to do what they did? If you were Brant, how would you have responded?

◄ Playback ►

1. What problem did the Loyalists create for the governor of Quebec?

2. Why did the Loyalists want Quebec to be divided in two? What benefits do you think this had for the English Loyalists? What benefits do you think this had for the French colonists?

3. Why do you think the British rewarded Butler's Rangers after the war but betrayed the Six Nations?

The Back Story

The Loyalists found a climate and way of life in British North America that was much different from what they were used to in the Thirteen Colonies. It was even harder, though, for the black Loyalists. Not only did they endure physical hardships. They faced **prejudice** and **discrimination** as well.

The Goal

Assume the role of either a young white or a young black Loyalist in the 1780s. Record your thoughts and feelings about your experiences in your new homeland in a series of journal entries.

The Steps

1. Before you begin, review the text and illustrations in this chapter to help you think of ideas. Then, do further research on the Loyalists in the library or on the Internet. View the first half of Episode 5, "A Question of Loyalties," in the video series *Canada: A People's History*.
2. Include at least five half-page journal entries from different periods and events in your early days in your new home.
3. Create sketches or illustrations to support your journal entries.

Evaluating Your Work

These are the criteria you should think about as you complete your work. Your work should:
*   clearly convey your thoughts and feelings
*   present accurate information
*   be neatly and clearly written
*   present illustrations that show your thoughts from your journal

History in Action

A Loyalist's Journal

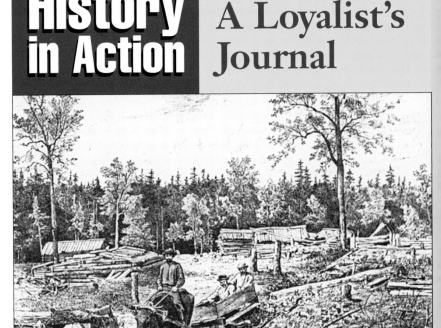

What were some of the hardships the Loyalists faced? How would you have reacted to these hardships?

CHAPTER 3

THE RED RIVER SETTLEMENT

Thomas Douglas was a wealthy Scottish noble known as the Earl of Selkirk. In Scotland and Ireland, greedy landlords were forcing poor tenant farmers from their land. Lord Selkirk wanted to help these poor farmers. He came up with a plan to resettle these peasant families in British North America.

Selkirk found land in the fertile Red River region of present-day Manitoba. The Hudson's Bay Company controlled the land. Selkirk wanted it, so he began to buy up **stock** in the company. By 1811, he owned a third of the Hudson's Bay Company's shares.

Now Selkirk had power and influence and he used these to obtain 300,000 km² of land along the Red River. It was a huge territory, five times the size of Scotland. Selkirk called the territory Assiniboia.

Lord Selkirk chose the Red River area to begin a colony for poor Scottish and Irish farmers. What do you think would have attracted Lord Selkirk to this particular area?

Scale

0   500 km

British Possessions

The place where the immigrants first settled was at the junction of the Assiniboine and Red Rivers. Today, this is downtown Winnipeg.

RECRUITING THE SETTLERS

Now that he had land, Selkirk needed settlers. In Scotland, he advertised the benefits of the Red River settlement—rich, fertile soil in an unsettled land where the farmers would be free to build new lives. He did not tell them about the short growing season or the heavy floods that plagued the region, though.

In spite of Selkirk's advertisement, it was not easy to recruit settlers. One reason was because the North West Company placed its own ads to counter Selkirk's. They warned the farmers that the Red River was a wild and hostile place where many dangers awaited them. But the tenant farmers had no choice. They had been forced off their land to make room for sheep grazing, which was more profitable for the landlords. So in 1812, the first group of Scottish and Irish immigrants arrived along the shores of the Red River.

A Year-Long Journey

Landing of the Selkirk Settlers, Red River, 1812

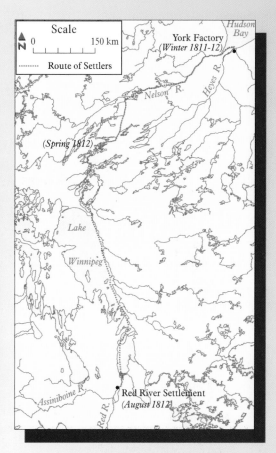

This map shows the route the settlers travelled from York Factory at Hudson Bay to the Red River settlement.

After a long and hazardous journey, the first settlers reached Red River in the summer of 1812.

A small group of settlers set sail for their new home in September 1811. By the time they reached Hudson Bay 61 days later, winter was setting in. It was too late to travel overland to Red River. So the settlers spent the winter in makeshift shelters 37 km west of York Factory. They survived on deer meat and **ptarmigan**. As winter wore on, many of the settlers became sick with scurvy. Aboriginal peoples had taught the Europeans some of their traditional medicines, though. They were able to cure the disease using tea made from the sap of white spruce trees.

In July, a small advance party set off for Red River. The settlement's new governor, Miles Macdonell, led the group. In August, they arrived at the junction of the Assiniboine and Red Rivers. Macdonell chose the west bank of the Red River to establish a settlement called Fort Douglas. A second group of settlers joined this group in October that same year.

What Was Pemmican?

Pemmican was made from dried buffalo or moose meat that was mixed with berries and fat, and then pounded flat. It kept for years without spoiling. Pemmican was a food staple for the fur traders.

Aboriginal peoples, the Métis, and the fur traders relied on the buffalo hunt. The buffalo had many uses besides providing meat to eat. Hides were made into moccasins, leggings, tunics, and winter coats. Tanned hides were made into tipis. The bones were carved into tools and utensils. The hair was braided into ropes and the sinew was used to make bowstrings.

SUSPICIONS ABOUT THE SETTLEMENT

When the settlers arrived, they were not welcomed by either the North West Company or the Métis. The North West Company believed the settlement was part of a plan to disrupt their fur-trading business. The settlement was right in the middle of their main trade route to the West. They needed this route to maintain the fur trade and to obtain provisions. Most of these provisions, including **pemmican**, were supplied by the Métis. They believed the settlers were a threat to their business, too. They were also worried that the settlers would drive away the buffalo, which was their main source of food.

HARD TIMES AT RED RIVER

The settlers faced starvation during their first winter at the Red River colony. To maintain a supply of food, they were forced to follow the buffalo herds as they migrated south. The settlers returned in the spring, but they had few farm tools and they were unable to harvest a crop.

The food shortage led to further suspicions on the part of the North West Company and the Métis. Then the governor of the colony, Miles Macdonell, issued the Pemmican Proclamation. This made it illegal to export food from the Red River area. This upset the North West Company even more. They needed to take food with them on their fur-trading expeditions. Now Macdonell was making it illegal to do so.

The Métis began burning the settlers' homes in an attempt to drive them out of the colony. The Saulteaux helped the settlers move to safety at a trading post at the north end of Lake Winnipeg. The settlers did not remain there, though. Later that year, they returned to Red River. When they did, Macdonell was arrested and the confrontations between the settlers and the Métis began again. By 1816, things were reaching the boiling point at Red River!

INCIDENT AT SEVEN OAKS

On June 19, 1816, a group of 61 Métis was travelling near the Hudson's Bay Company trading post of Fort Douglas. The group was led by a young man named Cuthbert Grant. They were carrying supplies for the North West Company. At a cluster of trees known as Seven Oaks, they were confronted by a group of 25 settlers from Fort Douglas. They were led by the new governor, Robert Semple. No one knows for sure what happened, but words were exchanged. Then shots rang out. In minutes, 20 settlers, including Semple, lay dead. The Métis lost only one man.

The conflict continued as the settlers' homes were burned to the ground. The next day, the settlers surrendered. They retreated once again to the trading post on Lake Winnipeg. Selkirk refused to give up, though. He sent troops to Red River. They seized the North West Company's Fort William and arrested several traders. Selkirk promised the settlers he would build them schools and churches if they returned to Red River.

From the Sources

Macdonell's Pemmican Proclamation in January 1814 increased the tensions at Red River.

No person trading Furs or Provisions within the Territory…shall take out any provisions, either of flesh or game or vegetables.

John Duncan Campbell of the North West Company responded to the Pemmican Proclamation. He urged the Métis to rise up against the colony.

Macdonell is now determined…to drive us out of the Assiniboia district and…out of the north west….You must assist me in driving away the colony. If they are not drove away, the consequence will be that they will prevent you from hunting. They will starve your families….

What Happened to Lord Selkirk?

The North West Company sued Lord Selkirk, claiming he had settled in Red River illegally. A long court battle followed that forced Selkirk into debt. In failing health, he finally abandoned the Red River colony. He moved to France, where he died in 1820 at the age of 48.

The incident at Seven Oaks marked the beginning of "the Pemmican Wars" between the Hudson's Bay Company and the North West Company.

The problems at Red River continued for a few more years. The rivalry between the North West Company and the Hudson's Bay Company threatened to shut down both businesses. Finally, in 1821, the two companies agreed to become one: the Hudson's Bay Company.

◄ Playback ►

1. (a) What factors pushed the Scottish and Irish tenant farmers from their homelands?
   (b) What factors pulled these immigrants to Red River?

2. Pretend you are an agent for Lord Selkirk. Create a poster to persuade Scottish tenant farmers to relocate to the Red River area.

3. What challenges did the colonists face as they travelled to the Red River? In your opinion, what would have been the greatest challenge? Why?

4. Assume the role of a newspaper reporter. Write an account of the incident at Seven Oaks. In your report, speculate on who fired the first shot and why.

THE CHALLENGES AT RED RIVER

Following the merger of the North West Company and the Hudson's Bay Company, peace finally came to Red River. But there was still one enemy the settlers could not defeat—nature!

The settlers had been plagued by poor weather since they first arrived at Red River. In 1818, however, the weather finally improved. The settlers had a plentiful crop. But before they could bring in the harvest, disaster struck! A cloud of grasshoppers descended on the settlement. The entire crop was destroyed. Once again, the settlers were forced to turn to the local Aboriginal people to help them survive the winter.

In 1819, the grasshoppers invaded again. This time, the damage was less severe and the settlers were able to harvest enough of their crops to keep them fed through the winter. But there were few seeds left for planting. So for the next couple of years, the farmers were unable to reap a full harvest.

THE DISASTERS CONTINUE

By 1822, the crop and harvest had rebounded. But nature still had more surprises for the settlers. In the fall of that year, flocks of birds found the harvest an appealing source of food, and they succeeded in eating most of the crop. Then, in 1823, the

In 1822, a census showed that there were 234 men, 161 women, 886 children, 126 houses, and 160 gardens in the Red River colony. Without Lord Selkirk's support, European settlers were no longer coming to the colony. Instead, the population grew as people who had lost their jobs in the fur trade settled in the colony.

Telling Their Stories

PEGUIS

The leader of the Saulteaux Nation, Chief Peguis, believed that his people could share the land with the settlers at Red River. His people helped the settlers avoid starvation and provided them with shelter when they first started their colony. Peguis still wanted to protect the interests of the Saulteaux, though, who had lived on the land for thousands of years.

View the clip "The Selkirk Settlers" (*Canada: A People's History*, Episode 6). What does Chief Peguis say about the land? Why do you think more settlers would doom the life of the buffalo hunters?

settlement was hit by drought. This was followed by severe hailstorms. Once again, the harvest was lost. In 1824, an early frost killed all the crops.

None of these disasters prepared the settlers for the events of 1825. First, spring floods led to a late planting season. Then a swarm of grubs and mice devoured most of the crops, while the wheat fields were destroyed by **fungus**. But the battle with nature was not over yet. In 1826, the worst flood in the history of the Red River colony washed away the settlement. Now the settlers had to start all over again.

Still, the settlers at Red River never gave up. They struggled on. Against all odds, they created the first permanent settlement on the Canadian prairies.

THE IMPACT OF THE RED RIVER COLONY

In time, the settlers at Red River overcame both conflict and hardship to build a successful colony. The settling of the region led to the end of the fur trade, though. Settlers and their farms now occupied the land where thousands of fur-bearing animals once roamed.

The colony also had a great impact on Aboriginal peoples. The Saulteaux were persuaded to sign a land treaty with the settlers. They believed the treaty was an agreement to share the land with the settlers. The settlers had other ideas, though. By signing the treaty, they believed the Saulteaux had given up any claim to the land. The settlers believed the land now belonged to them. When the Saulteaux realized what had happened, it was too late. They had lost the land they had lived on for thousands of years.

The arrival of the settlers also changed the Aboriginal peoples' way of life. They still hunted buffalo and other game, but many people began to farm, too. Then the **missionaries** came to Red River. They brought even more changes. They tried to **convert** Aboriginal peoples to the Catholic faith. They encouraged them to adopt European ways. The more settlers who came to Red River, the more life changed for Aboriginal peoples. Before long, their traditional way of life disappeared forever.

The Saulteaux were the original occupants of the land at the Red River colony. How do you think the people felt when their homeland was taken away from them?

◄ Playback ►

1. Imagine you are one of the Selkirk settlers facing the hazards of nature. Would you have stayed at Red River? Give reasons for your answer.

2. What qualities do you think a settler needed to survive at Red River? Give reasons for your answer.

3. Why do you think Aboriginal peoples and European settlers had different ideas about land ownership? Which idea do you support? Why?

The Back Story

Of all the challenges facing the Red River settlers, nature was the most difficult. The land contained rich soil that was ideal for farming, but nature always seemed to be working against the settlers. First, they had to adapt European farming methods to the short growing season. Then, they had to deal with the extremes of weather. Sometimes there was drought. Sometimes there was flooding. Occasionally, weather conditions were just right for farming. Then there were the insect plagues—grasshoppers, grubs, and locusts. The settlers battled all of these disasters as they worked to build a rich farming community along the Red River.

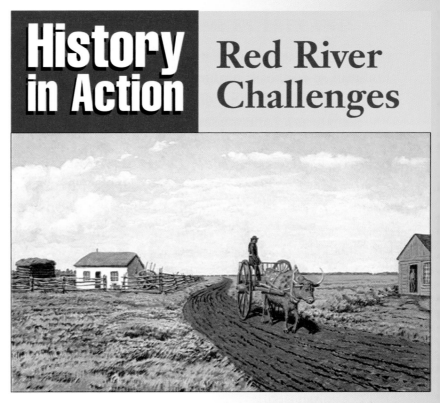

History in Action   Red River Challenges

What would you have found to be the hardest thing about life as a settler?

The Goal

Working with a partner, design and create a poster to illustrate one aspect of the hardships nature placed on the settlers. Your poster should have a theme about life in the Red River colony.

The Steps

1. Review the text and illustrations in this chapter. As you do, write down the challenges that the settlers faced.
2. Once you have a complete list, select a theme for your poster. Then identify the challenges that apply to that theme.
3. With your partner, brainstorm some ideas for designing and presenting your poster. Then do some rough sketches on a large piece of paper. Have a brief student-teacher conference to review your ideas.
4. If necessary after your student-teacher conference, revise your ideas. Then create the final product in a dramatic visual presentation. Add a slogan somewhere on the poster that reflects the theme.
5. Display the final poster alongside the other students' posters on a class bulletin board.

Evaluating Your Work

These are the criteria you should think about as you complete your work. Your work should:
- illustrate the challenges that are relevant to your theme
- be historically accurate
- use strong, colourful images
- include a slogan that catches the readers' attention

CHAPTER 4

THE IRISH MIGRATION

In the late eighteenth and early nineteenth centuries, farming was good in Ireland. Britain was fighting a war with France. It needed food to feed its large army and navy. This gave Irish farmers a ready market. They earned enough money to pay the rent to the English landlords. They even had a little left over for themselves.

Things changed when the war ended in 1815. Now Britain no longer needed a large army and navy, so they no longer bought food produced in Ireland. As a result, Irish farmers lost their British market.

During the Great Potato Famine in the nineteenth century, poor Irish farmers were forced to settle in North America. What hardships do you think they would have faced?

POVERTY AND HUNGER IN IRELAND

At the same time, the population in Ireland was growing quickly. Between 1801 and 1841, it doubled from 4 million to 8 million people. More people meant that more jobs were needed. So the landlords divided up the farms to make more farms to hire more workers. But the smaller farms made it hard for the farmers to produce enough food to pay their landlords and to feed their families. Poverty and hunger began to spread throughout Ireland.

In the early 1820s, Britain came up with a solution for what it called "the Irish problem." They decided to create settlements in British North America. Then poor Irish farmers could relocate there. And so a steady flow of Irish immigration to British North America began.

SETTLING IN NORTH AMERICA

The first Irish immigrants settled in the Maritime colonies. Eventually, however, they began to travel further west to settle in Upper and Lower Canada. Among the first to settle in Upper Canada was a group led by a man named Peter Robinson.

The Cholera Epidemic

In the 1800s, there were major epidemics in Britain and Europe. In 1832, Irish settlers coming to British North America brought one of these diseases with them: cholera. That summer, thousands of people became ill. Many people died. After this, the colonial government built a **quarantine** station at Grosse Île, 48 km from Quebec City. New immigrants were held there until officials were sure they did not have any diseases.

The quarantine station was built in 1832. For the next 15 years, officials there managed to avoid any major epidemics.

PETER ROBINSON'S IRISH SETTLEMENT

In 1825, Peter Robinson travelled to Ireland. He was looking to recruit settlers. He returned with over 2,000 Irish immigrants. They settled in an area of good farmland near Rice Lake in the eastern part of Upper Canada.

Peter Robinson became an immigration agent to encourage settlers to come to Upper Canada. Their first settlement was called Peterborough.

Once the ships reached Quebec City, the Irish immigrants travelled up the St. Lawrence River by boat. They camped out in the open on shore using bedding from the ships. They had only a few supplies and the clothes on their backs. It was a hard journey. The settlers had to row the boats. Then they had to carry them on their shoulders as they travelled parts of the route overland. It was too much for some of the settlers. After 18 months, 69 people had died.

Things did not get better when the group finally reached Kingston. Now they had to build a road for the supply wagons headed for Rice Lake. They also had to dig a deeper channel on the Otonabee River so larger supply boats could pass through.

By the time they reached Rice Lake, the settlers were too weak from physical exhaustion and disease to build their own shelters. So Peter Robinson hired other settlers to help them. The shelters were very basic—single-room huts made out of branches and mud. The huts were grouped together to resemble a small town. The settlers named their new home Peterborough, after Peter Robinson.

Moving on to the United States

Many Irish immigrants who came to British North America chose to move on to the United States. They did not want to remain within the **British Empire**. They had bitter memories of their former English landlords, who had shown little concern for their welfare back in Ireland.

A Smallpox Epidemic

Before leaving Ireland, the passengers were vaccinated against smallpox. But the vaccine did not work. Fifteen people died on the journey. Many others were infected with the disease. They were placed in quarantine at Grosse Île.

The Homes of the Irish

Like other immigrants, the Irish brought their culture with them. This could be seen in the homes they built. Irish homes in Peterborough reflected the style of the homes back in Ireland. The settlers made some changes, of course, to adjust to the climate and the building materials that were available to them. But the homes were still distinctly Irish.

These basic houses eventually disappeared. They were replaced with larger, better-built homes.

At first, they built basic shelters to protect them over the first winter in their new land. Then they replaced these shelters with modest homes made from stacked logs joined together at the corners. To make the roof, a log was split in half and hollowed out. Then the logs were laid alternately with the hollow side up, then down, in a gradual slope downward from front to rear. This created a trough that allowed water to flow down off the roof. The door was centrally located along the front wall, and there was a small window to provide a bit of sunlight inside. To create better protection against the weather, stacks of sod were laid against the outer walls.

Inside the typical Irish home, there was a large, three-legged iron pot. This was used for boiling potatoes and making stew. The pot was often a prized possession brought over from Ireland. In the kitchen, there was a hutch, a table, and some benches or stools. The bedrooms had beds with feather mattresses. There was often a rocking chair somewhere, reserved for a respected older member of the family.

BUILDING A LIFE IN PETERBOROUGH

The settlers were given a year's supply of medicine and food. They also received basic farm tools and cooking utensils. Each family was given a cow and some seeds.

The farms in Peterborough were much larger than the farms in Ireland. Larger farms meant that, in time, farmers were able to raise a variety of farm animals. These included cows, sheep, pigs, goats, horses, and oxen. They also planted a variety of crops, including wheat, oats, barley, peas, beans, turnips, and potatoes. They also grew hay to feed their animals.

The Irish suffered great hardships and lost loved ones along the way. Yet they still worked hard to build better lives for themselves and their families.

In time, the Irish built communities with schools, shop and churches.

◄Playback►

1. (a) **What factors pushed the Irish away from Ireland?**
   (b) **What factors pulled them towards North America?**

2. **What evidence is there that the Irish were able to build better lives in Upper Canada?**

3. **Imagine that you are one of the settlers who came to Peterborough with Peter Robinson. Write a letter to a friend back in Ireland describing your journey.**

A Bountiful Crop

Potatoes were a good crop for the Irish farmers. They could be produced in large quantities on limited amounts of farmland.

THE GREAT POTATO FAMINE

Meanwhile, back in Ireland, Irish farmers were about to face more hardships. The potato, a good source of vitamins and protein, was the most important food in the Irish diet. Potatoes helped to keep people well fed and in good health.

Then, in the 1840s, disaster struck! The potato crop was attacked by a deadly fungus. It caused the potatoes to rot and turn black. The **blight** spread throughout Ireland. Soon, the entire potato crop was wiped out. Between 1846 and 1849, **famine** swept across Ireland. At least 1 million people died from starvation and disease. Another million people left the country to come to North America.

English landlords forced the Irish tenant families from their homes. Then they destroyed the buildings so there would be no homes for the farmers to return to.

THE RESPONSE TO THE FAMINE

The potato famine created a crisis! But Britain was slow in offering help. In the meantime, the English landlords tried to make money. While the people of Ireland were starving, they sold millions of kilograms of food for export.

Finally, Britain introduced the Irish Poor Law to help the farmers. It created poorhouses to take in the poorest Irish farmers. The people received just enough food and warm clothing to survive. To pay for the poorhouses, the British government charged the English landlords a fee for any of their tenants who lived in them. The cost was £12 per person per year. But the landlords had an idea. It cost only £3 to £6 per person for passage on a ship to North America. So the landlords rounded up the tenant families who had worked their land and herded them on board ships bound for North America.

SHIPS CRAMMED WITH IMMIGRANTS

The shipping companies wanted to transport as many passengers as possible, as cheaply as possible. So they tried to cram in as many people as their ships would hold. To do this, they created

a special counting system. Passengers were labelled as statute adults. An adult male or female counted as one statute adult. A teenager, however, counted as half a statute adult. A child counted as only a third. So a family of seven— a mother, father, two teenagers, and three children— only counted as four people!

Passengers were crammed into the ships. How much room does this family have? How much privacy do you think they had?

When they could not pay the rent to their English landlords, the tenant farmers were **evicted**. These evictions were often harsh and without notice. Bridget O'Donnell tells how her family was evicted when they fell behind in the rent.

Dan Sheedy and five or six men came to tumble my house. They wanted me to give possession. I said that I would not; I had fever, and was within two months of my downlying [giving birth]; they commenced knocking down the house, and had half of it knocked down when two neighbours, women…carried me out. I had the priest and the doctor attend me shortly after….I was carried into a cabin and lay there for eight days, when I had the creature [child] born dead. I lay for three weeks after that. The whole of my family got the fever, and one boy thirteen years old died…with hunger while we were lying sick.

"Bridget O'Donnell and Her Children,"
London Illustrated News, 1849

Food was divided according to the passenger's status. A statute adult received a full **ration**. A teenager received only half a ration, and a child only a third. Often, the trip across the Atlantic took longer than expected. When that happened, the rations became smaller to make them last longer. As a result, there was not enough food. Most passengers were **malnourished**. This made them more likely to become ill with deadly diseases.

THE COFFIN SHIPS

On board the ships, the filthy and cramped conditions had deadly consequences. Many passengers were already sick with diseases such as typhus, cholera, and measles when they boarded the ships. In such close quarters, these deadly diseases spread quickly. Sick passengers were forced to remain on the lower decks of the ships. But it was still impossible to keep the diseases from spreading. Thousands of passengers died on the journey. As a result, these ships came to be known as the coffin ships.

THE GOVERNMENT INSPECTOR'S OFFICE

Those who survived the coffin ships were placed in quarantine once they reached Grosse Île. They had to remain there for long periods before they were allowed to settle in the colonies.

THE TYPHUS EPIDEMIC

The impact of the coffin ships and their deadly cargo reached Grosse Île on May 17, 1847. It was the beginning of a deadly typhus epidemic. It began after 200 passengers became ill only days after landing at Grosse Île. Then seven more ships arrived at the quarantine station later that week. At least 175 of the people on board the ships had died at sea. Another 341 were sick.

The quarantine station was not big enough to house all the passengers. Thousands of people were forced to remain on board the ships. Healthy people were forced to live alongside those who were sick. Officials at the quarantine station could do nothing to stop the disease from spreading. By the end of May, over 600 people had died on the ships and thousands more were sick.

Many patients had to be sent to hospitals in Quebec City. Soon, the hospitals were overflowing. There was fear and panic among the city's residents.

By June 5, 1847, 25,000 more people had arrived at Grosse Île. Almost 2,000 passengers had died at sea; 900 more had died after reaching the island. As the year wore on, the death toll grew. When the epidemic was finally over, 5,300 passengers had died at sea. Another 10,000 had died after arriving at Grosse Île.

From the Sources

Father Bernard McGauran was the chaplain at Grosse Île during the spring and summer of 1847. In a letter he wrote to the Archbishop of Quebec, he described the horrid conditions on board the coffin ships.

I hasten to give you a few notes on the very sad state of Grosse Isle. Tonight we can count seven hundred sick in the hospitals, all in desperate condition. Doctor Douglas does not want to receive any more on the island; since we truly have no place for them, he forces the captains to keep them on board, and we have at present thirty-two of these vessels which are like floating hospitals, where death makes the most frightful inroads, and the sick are crowded in among the more healthy, with the result that all are victims to this terrible sickness....

If we do not land the sick...we will need as many priests as there are ships.

Father Bernard McGauran,
Grosse Île, 24 May 1847

The Adoption of Irish Orphans

The deaths on the coffin ships left hundreds of Irish children orphaned. Many French settlers adopted these children. They allowed them to keep their Irish names. As a result, there are many French-speaking Quebeckers today with last names like O'Brien, O'Malley, and O'Neill.

In 1998, Parks Canada unveiled a monument to the Irish immigrants who had passed through Grosse Île during the epidemic.

By 1871, the Irish were the largest immigrant group in most large towns and cities in Canada outside of Quebec. Today, 13 percent of Canadians can trace their heritage back to Ireland. The Irish celebrate their heritage every March 17, in the St. Patrick's Day Parade in cities across Canada.

Telling Their Stories

D'ARCY MCGEE

D'Arcy McGee was an Irish immigrant who came to British North America in 1842. He was a politician and one of the founders of Confederation. He also loved literature and poetry. McGee wrote a novel, several history books, and he also wrote more than 300 poems.

In 1867, language and religion divided the new nation of Canada. McGee wanted to build a strong country based on mutual respect and tolerance between French and English Canadians. For D'Arcy McGee himself, however, this was not to be.

View the clip "From Sea to Sea" (*Canada: A People's History*, Episode 9, 16:04:25 to 16:13:02). Why do you think the Fenians branded McGee a traitor? What impact do you think McGee's murder might have had on Canada? Do you agree with McGee's belief that people can overcome their differences if there is mutual respect and tolerance? Give reasons for your answer.

◀ Playback ▶

1. Imagine you are a passenger on board one of the coffin ships. Describe your feelings during the ocean voyage and your quarantine at Grosse Île.

2. Often people believe that horrible things that happened in the past, such as epidemics, cannot happen today. Do you agree? Give reasons for your answer.

3. (a) In what ways did the adoption of Irish children whose parents died on the coffin ships demonstrate McGee's ideas about respect and tolerance?
   (b) In what ways can Canadians today show respect and tolerance for people of cultures and religions that are different from their own?

The Back Story

It is common in many cultures, including Ireland, for a family to create a coat of arms. The coat of arms records the family's history and that of their ancestors. A coat of arms contains many symbols. Shields, birds, animals, plants, and other symbols all have special meaning. The colours and lines on a coat of arms, and even the shape of the shield itself, have special meaning, too.

The Goal

Assume the role of an Irish immigrant who came to British North America during the Potato Famine. Create a coat of arms that tells the story of what happened to your family in Ireland and why you left your homeland to live in British North America.

History in Action

A Coat of Arms

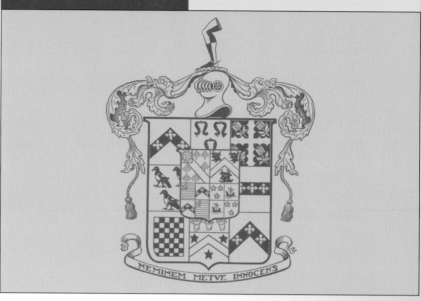

The Steps

1. Create an outline of the experiences of your imaginary Irish family during the Potato Famine.
2. Do some research into Irish coats of arms, either in the library or on the Internet. There are many books and Web sites that explain what the colours and symbols mean. Since there are hundreds of different symbols, limit your research to the most basic ones.
3. Choose colours and symbols that tell the story of your family's past and that reflect how you came to British North America.
4. Write a family motto that will appear in a banner along the bottom of your coat of arms.
5. Sketch a rough draft of the shield of your coat of arms. Discuss your ideas with a partner and exchange feedback before creating your final product.
6. Create a shield to display your colours and symbols. Then write a brief explanation of the meaning of the symbols and images.

What symbols can you identify on this Irish coat of arms?

Evaluating Your Work

These are the criteria you should think about as you complete your work. Your work should:

- show the experiences of your imaginary Irish family
- use appropriate colours and symbols to represent important events in your family's history
- be designed and presented in a colourful and creative way
- clearly explain the symbolism of your coat of arms
- be unique, personal, and imaginative

CHAPTER 5

FAST FORWARD

Long before Europeans arrived, North America was already culturally **diverse**. There were over 50 different Aboriginal cultures living across the continent. They spoke over 30 different languages. They practised many different lifestyles.

Then Europeans came to North America. First the French, and then the English, settled in what would become Canada. They brought their cultures, traditions, and values with them. Together, these cultures laid the foundations of a **multicultural** nation.

Since these early days of settlement, Canada has experienced many waves of **migration**. At first, most immigrants came from Britain and northern Europe. Then, as Canada expanded, immigrants from other parts of Europe came, too. Later in the twentieth century, Canada opened its doors to immigrants from all parts of the world—Asia, Africa, the Middle East, the Caribbean, and Central and South America.

In 1950, the population of Canada grew mainly because of the number of children who were born. This is called the birth rate. This is no longer true. Today, half of all population growth in Canada is the result of immigration. What do you think would happen to Canada's population if immigrants stopped coming here?

EQUITY
RESPECT
HARMONY
PROSPERITY

Diversity our Strength

🏛 TORONTO

Toronto is Canada's largest city. It is also one of the most multicultural cities in the world. Today, people from many countries around the world live in Toronto. What message do you think the city's motto sends?

ONE SOCIETY, MANY CULTURES

Today, Canada is a multicultural society. Canadians speak many languages and practise many religions. They celebrate many different cultural traditions. The desire to maintain their cultural identity is one reason immigrants choose to live in Canada.

Canada is a peaceful country. This does not mean that there are never any tensions between cultures, though. All people need time to adjust to changes in their societies. To help everyone adjust, people in Canada are encouraged to talk about their differences. If there are problems, they try to find solutions that serve the interests of all Canadians.

THE VALUE OF DIVERSITY

Immigration is important to Canada. When people from other countries come here, they bring new ideas with them. These ideas help make Canadian businesses more creative and competitive.

Without immigration, Canada's population would drop. This would be bad for the economy. There would not be enough workers to fill all the jobs. There would not be enough workers paying taxes. Without taxes, governments would not have enough money to provide Canadians with our high **quality of life**. So immigration benefits not only the country, but also all Canadians.

Immigration also creates economic links with other parts of the world. This helps to expand the markets for Canadian goods and services around the world. It encourages companies to invest money in Canada. This is important in today's **global economy**.

A Timeline of Multiculturalism in Canada

1971:   Canada becomes the first country in the world to adopt a policy of official multiculturalism.

1982:   Multiculturalism is recognized in the Canadian Charter of Rights and Freedoms.

2002:   The government announces that June 27 each year will be Canadian Multiculturalism Day to celebrate Canada's rich cultural heritage.

Having a diverse society has helped Canadians learn to listen to and respect the views of others. This gives Canada an important role to play in world affairs. Canada is often asked to help solve conflicts between groups of people in places around the world. Most Canadians are proud that Canada is a country that tries to solve some of the world's problems.

The goal of multiculturalism is to give everyone an equal voice. Canada is proof that it is possible for people of many races, languages, religions, and cultures to live together peacefully.

Fifty years ago, most immigrants to Canada came from Britain, Europe, and the United States. Today, most come from China, India, the Philippines, Hong Kong, and other parts of Asia. From what part of the world did your family originally come?

Healing the Past

Canada has not always accepted differences among people. Throughout our history, there have been many times when groups of people have been treated unfairly. This is what happened to the first inhabitants of North America.

For many years, Canada did not respect the rights of Aboriginal peoples. They made agreements with them. Then they failed to honour the agreements. In the process of building the nation, Aboriginal peoples lost their land and their rights. Their cultures were damaged by rules that were placed upon them.

Today, Aboriginal peoples want to reclaim their lands and regain their rights. They want to restore their cultures and preserve their heritages. For Canada to be a truly multicultural society in which all cultures are equal, Aboriginal peoples must find a sense of belonging.

The Census Tells the Story

A census is held every five years. It tells the government what population **trends** are happening in the country. The government wants to know such things as:

- From what countries and regions do immigrants come?

- In which provinces and cities do immigrants settle?

- How many children are born in Canada each year?

- How much is the population growing?

The answers to questions like these help the government decide what to do to keep the country strong and growing.

The Census Reveals...

In 2001, Canada took a new census. The results showed that population growth in Canada was at its lowest level ever—only 4 percent a year. This is much different than it was 40 or 50 years ago. Back in 1961, for example, the rate of population growth was almost 14 percent.

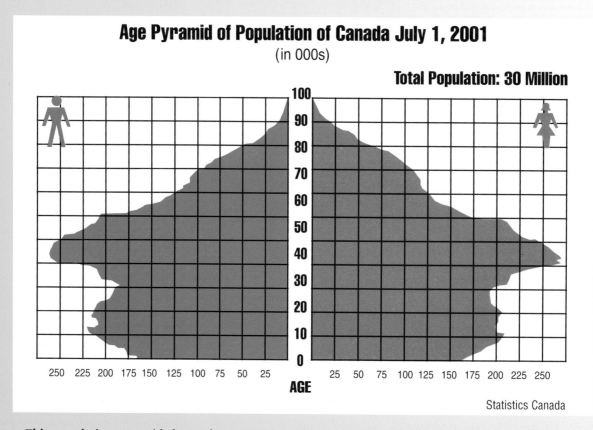

Age Pyramid of Population of Canada July 1, 2001

(in 000s)

Total Population: 30 Million

Statistics Canada

This population pyramid shows the age pattern of Canadians in 2001. How can you tell that the birth rate is going down—that is, that fewer children are being born?

Population Facts

The figures on the right are the population statistics for Canada between July 1, 2001, and June 30, 2002:

What was the *natural increase*—that is, the difference between the number of births and the number of deaths? What was the *net migration*—that is, the difference between the number of immigrants who came to Canada and the number of emigrants who left Canada? What do these figures tell you about population growth in Canada today? What does this say about the importance of immigration in Canada today?

Births:	327,187
Deaths:	231,232
Immigrants:	255,888
Emigrants:	71,042

Statistics Canada

◄Playback►

1. The following table lists the top eight countries of origin for immigrants to Canada in 1961 and 2001. On a blank outline map of the world, identify and label each country. Then, using different-coloured markers for each year and a legend, draw arrows from each country of origin to Canada. What patterns can you identify on your map?

Countries of Origin, 1961	Countries of Origin, 2001
1. Britain	1. The People's Republic of China
2. Italy	2. India
3. The United States	3. The Philippines
4. Portugal	4. The Special Administrative Region of Hong Kong
5. Greece	5. Sri Lanka
6. The Federal Republic of Germany	6. Pakistan
7. Caribbean States	7. Taiwan
8. Yugoslavia	8. The United States

2. Use what you have learned about immigration and settlement in this book to support the following statement: *Canadians are, by virtue of history and necessity, open to the world.*

(Prime Minister Jean Chrétien, 2000)

3. Create a motto that promotes the benefits of cultural diversity for Canadians. Display your motto on a colourful poster.

The Back Story

There have always been factors that push people away from their homelands and pull them towards another place. People may be pushed away from their homeland for many reasons. They may not be able to own land or find a job. Or perhaps there is a war going on or their home has been destroyed by a natural disaster. Or they may not be able to live freely or practise their own religion. These are some factors that lead to emigration.

People may be pulled towards a country for many reasons, too. There may be a better chance of finding a job or buying a farm. Or perhaps they are drawn to a place because it is peaceful and does not threaten their safety. Or maybe they are pulled towards a place because they can be free to practise their religion and express their opinions. These are some factors that lead to immigration.

History in Action
A Push-Pull Analysis

SETTLERS	PUSH FACTORS	PULL FACTORS	MY THOUGHTS

The Goal

For each group of immigrants discussed in Chapters 1, 2, 3, and 4, complete a chart outlining the factors that pushed them away from their homeland and pulled them towards Canada.

The Steps

1. Draw a chart similar to the one shown above, or create a chart on your computer.
2. Review the chapters in this book. For each chapter, make brief notes to record the push and pull factors that influenced each group of immigrants.
3. Select the key push and pull factors for each group and record them in your chart.
4. Write one or two paragraphs summarizing the conclusions you have reached about immigration to Canada.

Evaluating Your Work

These are the criteria you should think about as you complete your work. Your work should:
- highlight the important push and pull factors
- record information that is historically accurate
- be neat and complete
- be clearly written without spelling or grammar errors

Glossary

archaeologist a person who studies the past by looking at remains left at historic sites

assimilate to make a minority group of people practise the customs of a larger group

blight a harmful or destructive force

British Empire Britain's overseas colonies from the seventeenth century to the middle of the twentieth century

census an official count of a population

convert to change a person's beliefs

creation story the beliefs a people have about how they came to be on earth

democracy a state in which the government is elected by the people

discrimination treating a person differently because of race, gender, age, or religion

diverse varied or different

dowry money or property given by a bride's family to her husband

epidemic the widespread outbreak of disease in a community

evicted to be removed from a property

famine an extreme shortage of food

fungus an organism that feeds on other plants

global economy the world economic market for labour, capital, goods, and services

malnourished suffering from a lack of important foods needed for good health

migration movement from one place to another

missionary a person sent by the Church to spread religion

mob mentality the state of mind of a disorderly crowd

monopoly the control of a business by one person or group

multicultural preserving a number of distinct cultures within a unified society

naturalist a person who studies natural history

neutral not supporting either of two opposing sides

pemmican a food made from dried meat, fat, and berries, pounded into paste

prejudice a fixed opinion that is not based on the facts

primary industry an industry based on natural resources

ptarmigan various game birds of the Arctic

quality of life the standard of living and non-material things that people have

quarantine to isolate people who have come from other places in case they are carrying a disease

ration a fixed amount of food a person is allowed

refugee a person seeking shelter from danger or trouble

sabotage to deliberately damage or destroy something

self-sufficient the ability to supply one's own needs

siege an act in which an attacking army surrounds a place to cut off its supplies

staple a raw material such as fish, wheat, or timber

stock shares in a business

tenant farmer a person who farms rented land

traitor a person who betrays his or her country

trend the general direction in which something is going

world view a group's view of the world and its relationship to it

Index

Credits

Cover photo: Battle of Seven Oaks, 1816 by Charles W. Jeffreys. HBCA P-378 (N87-8) c. Hudson's Bay Archives; bottom right: *CBC, Canada: A People's History*; left: C. W. Jeffreys, Ontario Government Art Collection, C-096361; Page 1: Musée de Sainte-Anne-de-Beaupré; Page 2: SuperStock; Page 3: National Archives of Canada, C-013950; Page 4: Map, Paperglyphs; Page 5 top: Courtesy of Views of the Famine; bottom: Rochester Museum and Science Center (MR 545); Page 6: National Archives of Canada, C-082741; Page 7: Map, Paperglyphs; Page 8: CBC, *Canada: A People's History*; Page 9: La Nuova Francia by Giacomo Gastaldi, 1556. From Navigationi et Viaggi, Vol.3, by Giovanni Buttista Ramusio; Page 10: Toronto Public Library (TPL JRR4577); Page 11 top left: Nation Archives of Canada, C-003921, bottom right: SuperStock; Page 12 left: Courtesy of the Department of National Defence, right: National Archives of Canada, C-013950; Page13: CBC, *Canada: A People's History*; Page14: C.W. Jeffreys, National Archives of Canada, C-010688; Page 15: National Air Photo Library; Page 16: Canadian Heritage Gallery; Page 17: National Archives of Canada, C-073589; Page 18: National Archives of Canada, C-036647; Page 19: National Archives of Canada, C-000359; Page 20: National Archives of Canada; Page 22: National Archives of Canada, C-075208; Page 23: National Archives of Canada, C-001829; Page 24: Mary Evans Picture Library; Page 25: National Archives of Canada, C-005415; Page 26: The Granger Collection; Page 27: Map, Paperglyphs; Page 29: National Archives of Canada, C-000168; Page 30: Courtesy of Laird Niven; Page 31 top: Nova Scotia Archives and Record Management, right: National Archives of Canada, C-40162; Page 33: Map, Paperglyphs; Page 34 top: C.W. Jeffreys, Ontario Government Art Collection, C-096361, right: Map, Paperglyphs; Page 35: CBC, *Canada: A People's History*; Page 36: National Archives of Canada, C-061557; Page 37: National Archives of Canada; Page 38: Map, Paperglyphs; Page 39 left: J.E. Schaflein, HBCA P-388(N11312) Hudson's Bay Company Archives, right: Map, Paperglyphs; Page 40: Running Buffalo by Paul Kane, ROM 912.1.26; Page 41: National Archives of Canada, C-001932; Page 42 left: Provincial Archives of Manitoba PAM1987/363-p-80-s/6, right: Battle of Seven Oaks, 1816 by Charles W. Jeffreys. HBCA P-378 (N87-8) c. Hudson's Bay Company Archives; Page 43: National Archives of Canada, C-008714; Page 44: CBC, *Canada: A People's History*; Page 45: A Souteaux Indian, Travelling with his Family in Winter near Lake Winnipeg by H. Jones, (c. 1825). HBCA P-181(N14515c); Page 46: National Archives of Canada, C-013965; Page 47: Courtesy of Views of the Famine; Page 48: National Archives of Canada, C-120285; Page 49: National Archives of Canada, C-003350; Page 50: National Archives of Canada, C-011811; Page 51: National Archives of Canada, E000996222; Page 52: Courtesy of Views of the Famine; Page 53: National Archives of Canada, C-073435; Page 54: Courtesy of Views of the Famine; Page 55: ILN.1847/DRBSC, McGill University; Page 56 top: Parks Canada/Hélène Boucher, right: Clifford Skarstedt/CP Photo Archive; Page 57: CBC, *Canada: A People's History*; Page 58: The Granger Collection, New York; Page 59: Jonathan Hayward/CP Photo Archive; Page 60: City of Toronto; Page 61: Aaron Harris/CP Photo Archive; Page 62: Adapted from the Statistics Canada website http://www.12.statcan.ca/english/census01/Products/Analytic.Index.cfm.

Reviewers

Kathryn Brownell, Terry Fox School, Toronto, Ontario

Manny Calisto, West St. Paul School, West St. Paul, Manitoba

Greer Coe, Montague Intermediate School, Montague, Prince Edward Island

Rick Elliott, John Buchan School, Toronto, Ontario

Sheri Epstein, Langstaff High School, Thornhill, Ontario

Christine Greene, Avalon East School Board, St. John's, Newfoundland

Joanne Wheeler, St. Margaret School, Calgary, Alberta